THE MARKETPLACE GUIDE TO

OAK FURNITURE

THE MARKETPLACE GUIDE TO

OAK FURNITURE
Styles & Values

PETER S. BLUNDELL

Design CATHERINE THURO

THE MARKETPLACE GUIDE TO
OAK
FURNITURE
Styles & Values

ISBN 0-89145-141-2

Additional copies of this book may be ordered from:

Collector Books,   OR   Thorncliffe House Inc.
Box 3009,   4 William Morgan Dr., Thorncliffe Park,
Paducah, Kentucky 42001   Toronto, Ontario M4H 1E6

$17.95   ($19.95 in Canada)
Add $1.00 for Postage and Handling.

Design by Catherine M. V. Thuro
Typeset in Souvenir Light by Canada Stamp
Color separations by Colour Separations of Canada Ltd.
Printed and bound in Canada by The Bryant Press Ltd.

Published simultaneously in Canada by Thorncliffe House Inc.

Published by

Collector Books
Box 3009
Paducah, Kentucky 42001

To
Marian, Susannah and Fraser

Introduction

The idea of this book was established with the knowledge that prior to the 1870's there was a considerable amount of good, and sometimes great quality oak furniture already in existence on the North American Continent. Much of this earlier furniture has already been well documented by scholars I revere.

Unless specifically noted, and with the exception of captions that describe a particular piece, I include elm and ash woods when I refer to oak furniture. Today as in the days of its production, *oak furniture* is to some extent a generic term used to describe most of the furniture in this book.

This book is aimed at filling a void in our historical mosaic; and deals with that era of industrial revolution that saw furniture making evolve from a hand skill into an almost totally mechanized task. This era has been largely overlooked in the past because of general opinions about later furniture which did not allow it a place in the world of antiques. Magazines of the 1930's considered the collection in these pages to be merely "used furniture". More recently it has been branded "commercial furniture" by the people who have been greatly influenced by the 1930's

way of thinking. Large numbers of respected professionals, both on the curatorial side and the dealing side, agreed that the subject of "oak furniture" was definitely not for examination by scholars of antiques — *that is until recently.*

It is my belief that the label "commercial" is not altogether incorrect, for little of the oak furniture under observation in this book was entirely handmade, without some application of the assembly-line principle. This furniture was primarily made for "commercial" purposes to be sold in quantity, and to this extent it reflected market trends of the times. The boom in the production of furniture taxed the ingenuity of both established manufacturers and innovators to keep coming up with new ideas, or adaptations of old ones, that would satisfy a fast-moving and demanding market.

The buying and selling of oak furniture, long ignored by so many, is highly active at antique shows and shops, and every year becomes more acceptable. This acceptance has pointed up the need for a book that will show the wide variety of furniture of oak and similar woods that is available today. In doing this, the range of styles and designs illustrated should benefit those interested in interior decoration as well as those choosing furniture for restorations of this later period.

Strong recognition of, and demand for oak furniture, will have the same effect on its accessibility and availability, as did the recognition of furniture from the previous periods in earlier days. If one reflects upon the considerable amount of country furniture with original paint that was plentiful in the not-too-distant past, and compares that abundance with the dearth in today's market, then one can expect that the future of the furniture pictured here may well be the same.

Most previous books on oak furniture have dealt with the subject in line drawings from old catalogs, or in black and white photographs. This book deals with the oak furniture subject in all its living color. When one looks at the pictures on these pages, there is a feeling of amazement at all the colors and hues that are available, other than the popular golden oak finish. Golden oak is just one of many color treatments, and it is my belief that with the advantage of color photos in this book, we may discover the previously hidden beauty of lesser-known colors; and it is to be hoped that this will widen the spectrum of oak collecting and give pleasure to all the readers of this book.

When you read or "flip" through these pages, please bear in mind that the furniture was photographed at the "antique safari" level, and all the pieces were for sale at the time. Not one piece of furniture that appears here was found in a museum or a collection, even though the temptation to use those sources was ever present. The frustration that a collector must feel about "untouchable specimens" should be minimal in this book, for with a bit of good luck, observation, and good management, pieces of this caliber are still available in today's antique marketplace.
To help you to this end, find an antique dealer you like and trust — and do not wait too long until it's too late!

Acknowledgements

As we traveled, we made good friends and benefitted from the knowledge and hospitality of many. A sincere thank you to all of the following who helped in the project and who allowed us to take these colorful photographs.

My wife, Marian, who typed manuscripts, looked after our store and children single handed while I was away, yet still had enthusiasm for the whole project at the end.

Catherine and Carl Thuro, who guided my efforts every step of the way.

My father, Thomas Blundell, for his enthusiasm and accounting services.

Penny Savosh, we needed your help — a special thank you.

The Reid Girls Flea Market at Brimfield, Massachusetts, who allowed us to park our mobile studio on their market field for three days and gave us all the help we required and more. My thanks to Jill Reid Lukesh and Judith Reid Mathieu of "Antique Acres" and Fred Dole who helped when technical gremlins overtook our equipment.

George J. Silverman of Lawrence, Massachusetts for his kindness and a very extended "half hour". Also John and Mary Silverman for their great hospitality.

And also to:

Betty Adam, Tilbury, Ont.
Nancy Alan, Conway, Mass.
Patricia and Jim Alex, Worchester, Mass.
Seymour and Violet Altman, Clarence, N.Y.
Lindsay Anderson, Regina, Sask.
"Antique Andy", Revere, Pa.
Howard J. Arkush, Greenfield, Mass.
Jim and Teresa Barker, Proton Sta., Ont.
Molly Bartram, Toronto, Ont.
Michael Bucino, New York, N.Y.
Ray Chapman, Hammond, N.Y.
Dave Coghill, Newcastle, Ont.
Edward C. Collins, Walpole, Mass.
Bruce Cummings, Hadley, Mass.
John Espeland, Claremont, N.H.
Irene and Robert Faubert, Tilbury, Ont.
Royal F. Feltner, Amesbury, Mass.
Zella and Vic Goetz, Toronto, Ont.
Stephen Goetz, Toronto, Ont.

Tony Greist, Amesbury, Mass.
Cora Grunwald, Ledyard, Ct.
Marion Hagey, Toronto, Ont.
Harbourfront Pickers Market, Toronto, Ont.
William Hawkes, Toronto, Ont.
Linda Howard, Uxbridge, Ont.
Finella Hughes, Unionville, Ont.
Bill and Dot Kenny, Spencerport, N.Y.
Donna Kay and Jerry Keyer, Randall, N.Y.
Dave Law, Bailieborough, Ont.
Steve Lee, Manchester, N.H.
Joe MacDougall, Greenfield, Mass.
Liz and Charles Martin, Windsor, Ont.
Carol and Dick Morse, South Easton, Mass.
The Plaintainers, St. Catharines, Ont.
Gene Ploss, Grafton, Mass.
"Red" and "Bum" Porter, Moultonboro, N.H.
The Rays, Mansfield, Conn.
Ken and Lori Rifenburg, Madison, N.Y.
Ralph Rosetti, New York, N.Y.
Greg and Linette Salisbury, Skowhegan, Maine

The Sharkeys, Milliken, Ont.
Mark Smallacombe, Teeswater, Ont.
Herman Steckerl, Haverhill, Mass.
Henry Stevenson, Unionville, Ont.
David Stewart, Brooklin, Ont.
Robert Stewart, Lisbon, N.H.
Ron Sullivan, Georges Mills, N.H.
Sutherland Antique Showsales,
    Scarborough, Ont.
Tom Valentino, Cold Spring, N.Y.
Robert Watts, Elmira, N.Y.
John Wallick, Palmer, Mass.
Wimodausis Club of Toronto, Ont.
Ron Windebank, Toronto, Ont.
Betty Wolf, Westford, Mass.
John R. Wright, Toronto, Ont.
Paul Zammitt, Toronto, Ont.

The Marketplace - Past

The oak era in North America can be summed up as the age of catalog fashion. Fashion had for some time come from the written word; books such as Charles Locke Eastlake's 1868 *Hints on Household Taste* had formed opinions and started a trend. People of average means could read more and they avidly consumed the messages written in the periodicals of the day.

In the 1880's, the department store catalog was eagerly awaited by every consuming family on the Continent. It was in this mood that oak furniture flourished and reigned supreme for almost forty years until nearly all the massive stands of oak lumber had been exhausted.

The shape of much of this furniture was influenced by the catalog trade. A certain degree of standardization was necessary in order to crate and ship the merchandise at the lowest possible cost. Furniture was commonly crated intact from the factory and sent to the agent for any minor assembly before delivery. As time went on, the customer did his own uncrating and assembly.

Standardization of furniture sizes also went hand in hand with the construction of standard houses built during the oak period. The use of oak was popular for inside trim in houses so it was predictable that people moving into new houses at that time would choose oak furniture over all other woods.

The emphasis in the oak period was for strong unbreakable furniture contrary to the fussy fragility of a lot of the Victorian furnishings. As time went on designs became simpler and more austere, and this may be a consideration when dating oak furniture.

There are other ways of dating this furniture. The quality of wood available deteriorated and the stock sizes of the lumber grew smaller and less perfect as time rolled on. Cost-saving features were implemented such as thin panelled doors and sides, the use of veneers, and the laminating of three or four boards to make a top or drawer front. Towards the end of the era, other substitutions were made.

Plain woods such as maple were printed with false graining to simulate the grain of oak, and then colored to imitate the popular color of oak. These printed "fake" oaks still confuse the neophyte today.

Without exception, catalog companies such as Montgomery Ward, Sears Roebuck, and Eaton's in Canada shipped everywhere from Coast to Coast, and furniture found in every city, town, and village of North America reflects their influence. Thus to hundreds of thousands of people from all nations, this was the golden age of Americana.

The Marketplace - Present

Oak furniture was designed to appeal to large numbers of people of average means. It still holds this position today as pieces of oak are available to people of modest means as well as the well-to-do.

The nationwide acceptance of oak-type woods, and the furniture made from these woods, says much about the interest in our heritage and our pride in the past. Awareness of the oak furniture marketplace is something that has accelerated in the past ten to fifteen years.

To satisfy today's demands, cross-market migrations of furniture have been necessary to compensate for a lack of variety in some geographic areas. These migrations of furniture from State to State and Coast to Coast add to the excitement, interest and challenge for the dealers and collectors involved.

Geographically the marketplace is very diverse. On a trip across the country, I noticed that most of the furnishings in Midwestern and Western museums consisted of furniture that the average antique dealer sells today. We must remember, however, that we are a new continent and the mass furniture market of the oak era was indeed the true heritage period for more than two-thirds of the Continent. At the time of writing, the demand for oak furniture is greatest on the West Coast and the Midwest regions. The supply, however, largely comes from the North Eastern States and Canada.

To meet this market need, a complete network exists of "pickers" (people who buy at the house level) and "haulers" (those people who buy from the pickers in bulk). The store buyers or auctioneers usually buy from the haulers and try to find a proper final home for the furniture.

Major city centers such as Boston, Massachusetts; New York City; Houston, Texas; Los Angeles, California and Seattle, Washington and others are all host to many antique-related industries catering to the buying, selling, refurbishing and refinishing of furniture for today's marketplace. There are many professional paint and varnish strippers and as many refinishers and repair people. These men and women survive by their knowledge of woods and the trade in general, and they should be recognized for their ability to give an independent judgement regarding their own particular areas of expertise.

Large amounts of oak furniture go under the hammer at auction every week all across the country. Although auctions constitute an immediate source, they are an expensive place to learn the intricacies of the antique business. Auctions are for experts who already know their subjects: an expert can at an auction sometimes find a bargain or a piece that will complete his or her collection. This is not to say that beginners should not visit the auction hall, just remember that much furniture that has had extensive repair or restoration is sold at auction, and there is always an element of risk including that of discovering too late that a piece is inhabited by live wood borers. Remember the rules of the auction are "Caveat Emptor" or "Buyer Beware".

By far the best method of learning is to visit antique stores, shows, flea markets and museums. Do not be afraid to ask questions if your curiosity is aroused.

Price premiums are paid for signed pieces of furniture and one should be aware of the importance of original labels. Names such as Stickley, Roycroft and Hunzinger should send alarm bells ringing if found. Price premiums are also paid for pieces in good original condition; conversely you can generally expect to pay less for a piece hidden under layers of paint.

The oak marketplace is very fast-moving and you will find out that "he who hesitates is lost". When you find the piece of your dreams, if it passes close inspection and the price is in line, buy it and enjoy it.

"By Any Other Name"

The North American Continent is vast and regions differ immensely in language.
This section is devoted to different names given to articles in this book, keyed to the list of contents. If you are confused, I may not have caught all the local names:

Suites (Pr. sweets) - Suits (Pr. soots)

Ensemble - matching room setting

Bedroom - chamber

Dressers - dressing tables, princess dressers, toilet tables, bureau, commode (French)

Chiffoniers - high boys

Washstands - hotel stand, jug stand, towel stand, toilet stand, commode

Chairs - bentwoods, pressbacks, diners, dining chairs, "Vienna" chairs, parlor, sitting room, reading, students, arm chairs, rockers, rocking chairs

Bookcases - parlor and wall cabinets, book cabinets, library cases, book racks

Desks - rolltops (curtain desks), office desks, notedesks, parlor desks

Hall benches - settles, settees

Sideboards - buffets, servers, dining board

China cabinets - closets, cupboards

Tables - parlor, sitting room, tabourettes, jardinier stand, lamp table, parlor stands, dining, round, square, extension

Kitchen cupboards - kitchen organizer, "Hoosier" cupboard, bake table, kitchen helper

Ice boxes - ice chests, refrigerators

What-nots - novelty stands, bric-a-brac shelf

Remember also that *catalog* was often spelled *catalogue*.

Contents

This elaborately-ornamented bed is an
example of Victorian Renaissance furniture
circa 1875. It is typical of the flamboyant
decoration popular during the centennial
period. Most of the heavily-carved furniture
of this period was usually made of walnut or
mahogany. The effect was grand but not
lively. Sharply contrasting woods have given
this bedroom suite an exuberance that is a
refreshing change.

The towering headboard is 99" high. The
lady's face in the center looks down non-
committally, but the wolf-like pressings on
either side appear to be aggressively on
guard. The trophy-like decorations atop the
bedposts appear symbolic of the attainment
of material goals. Ash with burled-walnut
veneer panels and black walnut trim.
Original finish in excellent condition.
h. 99", w. 56"

a.

c.

(a) The dresser matches the bed on the previous page. The complete set also includes (b) an equally spectacular washstand. Both the dresser and the washstand have oil-lamp sconces in strategic places. Victorian "teardrop" pulls are the typical hardware for this style. (c) Detail of the bed siderail which is also decorated in its entire length with walnut carving and burled-walnut veneer. Siderails are sometimes replaced to extend the length to accommodate today's taller generation.
(a) h. 99", w. 50", d. 18".
(b) h. 44", w. 37", d. 18".

b.

a.

(a) This stylish cheval dresser would have probably come from a catalog furniture house. In the past the two-drawer dresser was sometimes separated from the cabinet and the mirror hung on the wall, however, the current trend is to keep these pieces intact. Ash. h. 77", w. 42", d. 18"

(b) This "side-by-side" cheval-mirror combination dresser has machine-carved applied trim and incised decoration. These pieces accommodated sloping ceilings in bedrooms. Ash. h. 71", w. 40", d. 17"

b.

a. Quarter-sawn oak veneer is predominant on these drawer fronts. This style of ladies' dressing table was very popular in the early 1900's. Applied machine-carved trim starts to diminish in importance in this period. The dropped middle shelf was to house milady's dresser set. Small stools were sold to go with these for her to sit upon whilst engrossed in beauty preparations. h. 68", w. 39", d. 21".

b. Another variant of the dressing table. These butterfly mirrors swung out to give the lady of the house a side-view peek at her coiffure. This version was made after 1910. It is a very rare occurrence today to find original keys, however, replacements are easily made. Note swell front and tiny paw feet. Oak. h. 54", w. 32", d. 20".

There is quarter-sawn oak veneer on the 'swell' front of this dresser.
The piece is interesting in detail having lion-paw feet with cabriole legs and
fancy fretwork on the mirror supports. The applied trim is machine carved as
was usual for the era. The quality of the mirrors was emphasized to catalog
readers and only the more expensive pieces sported "German" or "French"
bevel mirrors. In Canada the emphasis was on "British" bevel mirrors,
probably due to the British Imperial influence of the times.
h. 73", w. 46", d. 23".

a. The top drawers are oak veneered in this "swell-front" dresser, which is almost devoid of decoration.
h. 67", w. 39", d. 21".

b. This Edwardian dresser has hardly any fancy trim. Veneer-ply side panels and small size mirror all show attempts at cost savings.
Oak. h. 55", w. 34", d. 15".

c. The early 1900's dresser above has applied machine-carved trim. Top drawers are quarter-sawn oak.
h. 71", w. 40", d. 18".

d. The top surface and top drawer-fronts are veneered in this piece of oak. The light lines suggest that it was a lady's dresser. h. 67", w. 43", d. 21".

a.

(a) Refinished elm dresser with swing mirror having machine-carved applied trim.
Elm. h. 75", w. 38", d. 14".

(b) This dresser is fairly fancy. Notice the routing and the extra work on the mirror frame. The shelf would have been used for oil lamps, ring trees, hair receivers or brushes. Elm. h. 72", w. 36", d. 18".

Three-drawer dressers were a "must buy" for everybody who bought a bedroom suite from a catalog during the oak era. Although prices varied considerably with quality, the same basis for design existed for most dressers: three drawers, a swivel mirror, some form of trim for decoration and something common to a lot of these dressers — a 'double deck' — meaning a top surface made to look two layers thick. Rarely were these 'double decks' actually solid wood all the way through, rather the bottom deck was a frame upon which sat the top. To have had two solid decks would have been wasteful of wood and costlier to ship.

a.

"Swell" fronts on drawers were considered a new style in 1897. They started out slightly bowed and in time the swell became more prominent. Both steam-bent solid wood and veneered fronts were used.

(a) Four-drawer dresser or bureau with machine-carved applied trim and shaped top. The top two drawers have a rare figured hardwood veneer (possibly a burled ash). h. 74", w. 41", d. 22".

(b) The top drawers of this dresser also have an unusual hardwood-burl veneer. The carcass of the rest of the piece is solid elm. h. 74", w. 43", d. 20".

Brass hardware greatly adds to the value of a piece if it is original.

Unfortunately over the years hardware has a tendency to wear out or crack-up, however, replacements may be bought at antique shops or by mail order. Lock and keys seldom stay together so if you want a key for your lock, you will have to have one made by your local locksmith.

Wooden escutcheons (keyhole covers) were often made at the factory level as a by-product.

Wooden hardware usually indicated an economy piece because brass hardware would have been an outside purchase.

b.

a. Dresser with a variety of horizontal lines. Oak. h. 70", w. 40", d. 18".

b. Elm dresser trimmed with die-pressed carvings. h. 69", w. 36", d. 18".

c. This dresser from the early 1900's, features plain round 'bosses' and parallel lines. Oak. h. 69", w. 37", d. 18".

d. The less-common two-drawer dresser above is often referred to as a "princess" dresser. Oak. h. 69", w. 40", d. 17".

When furniture catalogs specified "antique" oak finish, this is what you would have received. Today this original finish is highly desirable to keep and it is quite conceivable that modern-day refinishers will soon be trying to imitate the effects. Notice the raised-panel drawer fronts and swivel-beveled mirror. Oak. h. 72", w. 43", d. 18".

A plain dresser or bureau. Notice the panelled sides. This was an attempt to lighten the piece for shipping and reduce wood costs by "thinning down" the sides. Applied machine carving adorns the top of the mirror. Elm. h. 72", w. 42", d. 19".

This example of a chiffonier shows how mass-produced machine-carved trim was used. The same motif trim was used twice in this case. The backboard has a fancy cut to it that dresses up an otherwise plain piece of furniture. Oak. h. 52", w. 31", d. 18".

Chiffoniers like these were essential to complete the well-furnished bedroom. They would have appealed mainly to the man of the house, and frequently the cupboard was used for storing shaving equipment. The small drawers would have more than likely been used as collar and cuff drawers for the stiffly-starched linen or celluloid collars and cuffs which were used by every well-dressed male in the early 1900's.

(a) This early 1900's chiffonier has tokens of styling in a modified cabriole leg and a small amount of machine-carved trim on the backboard. Shortly after this piece was made, furniture lines became straight and ornamentation disappeared altogether. Oak. h. 63", w. 31", d. 18".

(b) Distinctive design is embodied in this fine-quality five-drawer chiffonier. The backboard replete with beveled mirror, shelf and rolling-pin trim makes the piece interesting. Oak. h. 65", w. 31", d. 18".

(c) A superb example of a top-of-the-line chiffonier. Notice the quality of the wood. The right-hand side post is hinged to form a locking device, locking all drawers at once. The turned finials on the backboard add to its character. Oak. h. 62", w. 35", d. 20".

a.

b.

c.

A washstand was essential to complete a bedroom set before most houses were converted to contain upstairs bathrooms and indoor plumbing. The cupboard in these washstands was used to keep the water jug of the washset and the chamber-pot, both very necessary to home comfort. In days gone by, our ancestors had little heating in their houses, and in a Northern winter it would have been normal to "break the ice" before being able to wash.

a.

b.

(a) Washstands such as these are in heavy demand today and a slight premium is paid when the towel rack is still attached. Three drawers and one door with machine routed reeding also make an attractive combination. Elm. h. 45", w. 28", d. 16".

(b) A plain washstand with one drawer, one door. The three tongue-and-groove door panels are routed to make them appear to have six panels. Drawer pulls have stamped brass backplates. Elm. h. 33", w. 26", d. 17".

In this washstand, the raised panels, lapped drawers and heavy cast-brass hardware are all features sought after by collectors today. h. 53", w. 38", d. 21".

Lion-paw feet and a "swell" or bow front covered with quarter-sawn oak
veneer, are features of this washstand which matches the bed on the
opposite page. The towel bar is of the harp or lyre shape.
Oak veneer. h. 51", w. 34", d. 18".

This bed is probably the most striking example of the use of quarter-sawn veneer that we encountered in the antique marketplace at the time this book was written. The advantageous use of dark stain highlights the overall effect.
Oak. h. 75", w. 58".

Turn-of-the-century catalogs provide a look at the selling points promoted by the copy writers of the day. Strong emphasis was placed upon serviceability and long-term durability. The trim described as hand carved would be more accurately listed as machine-carved today.

Frequent reference was made to the attractive grain of wood, for example: "Choicest quarter-sawn oak, the grain stands out and adds very greatly to the elegance of the general appearance". Quotations such as this, and "the panels are all handsomely finished" were the enticements that encouraged customers to order huge quantities of furniture from the catalogs.

(a) Some people identify this bed with the "mission-oak" styling. Others call it "institutional". Whatever the category, these pieces are fairly hard to find and generally sell quickly today. Oak. h. 53", w. 55".

(b) Thick lumber was used in this massive bed. The machine-carved trim is reminiscent of castle-gate hinges. Oak. h. 54", w. 58".

(c) This bed has a small amount of machine/hand incising used as decoration. This style was a transition from Eastlake to Edwardian. Ash. h. 64", w. 56".

a.

b.

c.

Currently the fine lines of this bed are not as popular as they should be. It has been suggested that oak collectors only appreciate the heavier look. Taste is purely personal but I really like this one. Oak. h. 78", w. 57".

a.

(a) Beds like this are both hard to find and expensive when you do come across them. The use of quarter-sawn oak in the panel on the headboard is attractive. Although the major part of the bold trim was machine carved and applied, some of the irregular pieces needed to be custom carved. Oak. h. 76", w. 64".

(b) The applied carving on the headboard shows an attempt to use the inspiration and lines of the *Art Nouveau* phase. Ash. h. 78", w. 57".

(c) This Eastlake-style bed has painted panels that simulate birds-eye maple. The use of stains to darken the trim is effective. Elm. h. 76", w. 55".

b.

c.

The magnificent bed above has the unusual combination of black stained incised carving and applied carved trim. It was probably custom made. The grain of the wood has obviously been selected and carefully placed to gain the quarter-sawn tiger-stripe effect on the panels. Oak. h. 73", w. 59".

The chairs in this section vividly reflect the great variety of styles the manufacturers produced in oak, elm and ash during the last half of the 19th century, and into the early years of this century. Although the bulk of production consisted of styles illustrated in the catalogs of this period, there are many pieces that are variations of, or complete departures from the mail-order examples. Some of the chairs included here are possibly more compatible with furniture made of other woods such as walnut or maple, than they are with typical catalog furniture.

You may wish to use a single chair as an interesting accent in a room, or two or more of a kind at a dining table. When shopping for the latter it should be kept in mind that the cost per chair generally increases with the number of like ones available.

Many features are combined to make this an attractive and interesting chair. Relatively clean lines accentuate the ornate carving at the top of what is known as a keyhole back. The shaped seat and cabriole legs with lion-paw feet denote strength and grace in this solid oak piece.

(a) This unusual adaptation of a much earlier chair shows many Windsor-style features in the seat, back supports and cross stretchers. Original Windsor chairs are exceedingly rare and command a high price.

a.

(b) An excellent example of a turn-of-the-century "Roman" chair, listed in the Montgomery Ward 1897 catalog as "The proper thing for odd parlor or window piece, also for hall use". Note the cherubic face on the back and the lion-paw feet.

b.

In the 1897 Sears Roebuck catalog, a similar chair was described as a "corner chair". Although not the typical three-legged triangular corner chair, the placement of the back legs would better adapt the chair to a corner. Oak.

(a) A peculiar shape in an oak chair. This almost barrel-like chair combines a bent-wood hoop stretcher with fancy cut arm rests and back. Note how the hoop goes through the front three legs and inside the back.

a.

b.

(b) A plain oak side chair that would go well with Mission-oak furniture. If you look closely you can see the horizontal 'tiger-stripe' lines of the quarter-sawn oak back splat. The seat is shaped for comfort. Many earlier chairs had hand-planed or hewn shaped seats, however, from the great numbers of shaped-seats in existence today that were made in the oak era, it seems apparent that new machinery techniques were developed at that time, to speed up the process.

a.

(a) Sears Roebuck sold bent-wood chairs of similar construction to this in 1897 and called them "Vienna" diners after Thonet, the Vienna, Austria manufacturers. Chairs made of bent-wood could be shipped directly to the customer in "knocked-down" condition. In today's marketplace the influence of Michael Thonet is not generally known and most chairs of this nature are now simply called "bent-woods". In the catalog of 1897 these chairs were said to be made of 'rock elm', although later catalogs just refer to them as 'hardwood'.

(b) There are characteristics in this chair of the *Art Nouveau* style of the early 1900's. It is an interesting dining chair from a period that generally produced plain furniture without ornamentation. Oak.

(c) Functional and sturdy mission-style oak dining chairs such as this were extremely popular in the post-1915 period until the late 1920's. Some of these chairs were caned (this one has been newly caned), or seats could have been chosen to be upholstered. Notice how by this time almost all dining chairs had 'box seats'. This gave a strong substantial look to any chair.

b.

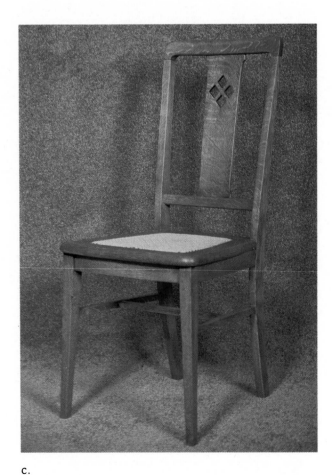

c.

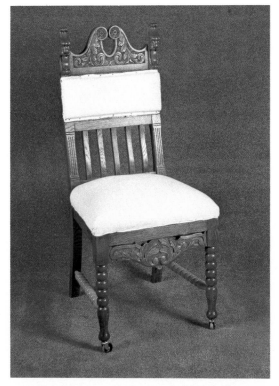

a. A heavily-carved chair with lions carved on the back posts. The seat is ready to receive replacement upholstery. Oak.

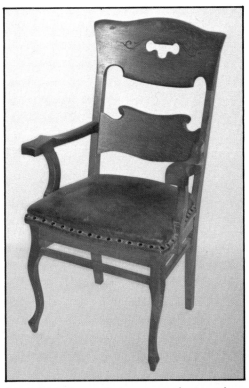

b. A fairly fancy dining-room chair, with incised carving around the hole in the back. Note the shaping on the solid arms, back and French-style cabriole legs.

c. This dining chair has bent-wood-style splayed legs and intriguing barleytwist spindles in the back. Oak.

d. Mission-oak arm chair. Notice the use of quarter-sawn grain to enhance a plain style. When you see this type of chair, start looking for evidence of trade marks or stampings.

Pressback chairs are the epitome of the catalog-furniture era, and of low-cost, mass-produced wood furniture that gave the impression of hand-made quality. To this end some examples succeeded more than others, particularly those that had been completed with some hand-chasing or chiseling.

The backs of these chairs were generally bent or shaped with the use of steam. Heat, tremendous pressure and a metal die were necessary to press or emboss the design into the wood. The amount of pressure and the design of the die, were important factors that affected the degree to which the wood was forced into the cavities of the die, hence the degree to which the design *appeared* to be carved.

a.

b.

(a) Sir Wilfred Laurier was a popular Prime Minister of Canada, and this elm pressback chair was made to commemorate his office in 1896. A number of other pressback character chairs was made depicting such famous figures as Queen Victoria and King Edward VII of England. There is one with a mythical Greek goddess, and several of the "Old man winter" or the North wind, West wind or East wind.

(b) This attractive cane seat pressback armchair has bent-wood single post back legs. The bent-wood influence also shows under the armrests in the support brackets. Note the small apron under the seat to give the thin cane seat a more substantial appearance. The three-rung stretchers are a small indication of extra quality. Oak.

In the past, many antique dealers and collectors were disdainful of articles that were mass produced, or were less than one hundred years old. Pressbacks are among those now accepted by all who recognize the significance of articles which reflect our past.

a.

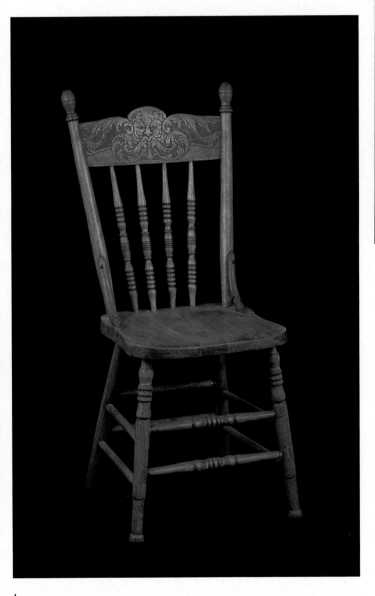

b.

(a) The delicate lines of this pressback armchair and the general lightness of the design would indicate that it was made to appeal to women. The fancy pressed back rail and its two small cameo medallions are an unusual treatment for a pressback chair. Although this chair does not have a Windsor-style seat, there are slight traces of Windsor influence in the seat and the H-stretcher. The turned back spindles are very long in comparison with other turnings from the 1890's.

(b) The west wind puffs out from the die-pressed back of this elm pressback kitchen chair. Mail-order catalogs usually called pressbacks "dining chairs" or "diners", and the term "kitchen" chair was only used for the least expensive of their offerings. Chairs with taller backs would usually have been bought for the dining room.

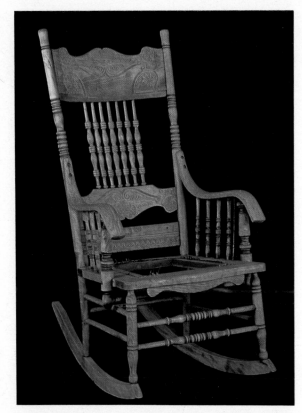

a. All three back slats with pressings, is the most unusual feature of this elm rocker.

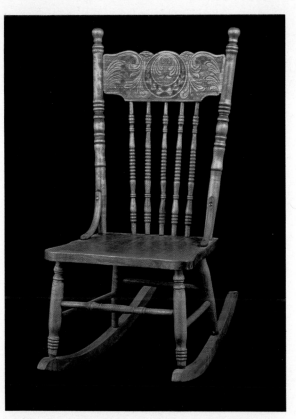

b. The low seat and lack of arms qualify this pressback chair as a 'nursing rocker'. Elm.

c. Laminated wood was used for the seat of this rocker. Elm.

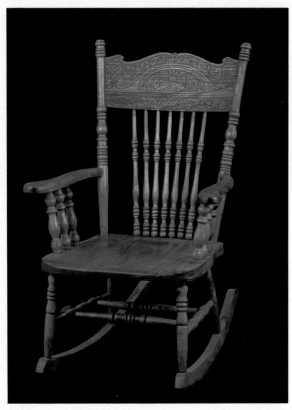

d. The pressing of the pattern on the back of this elm chair is quite shallow.

a. Mushroom-cap finials, stick-and-ball lattice work, the incised back rail, heavy turnings and a box skirt indicate this was a top-of-the-line chair. The seat has an oak veneer. Oak.

b. Fanciful fretwork is combined with machine carving on a steam-bent laminated back to produce this interesting oak rocking chair. Like (a) the seat has an oak veneer.

c. The quarter-sawn veneered back and roll-front seat were steam-bent to follow body contours. Oak.

d. The square lines of a mission chair are combined here with machine-carved applied trim and quarter-sawn oak.

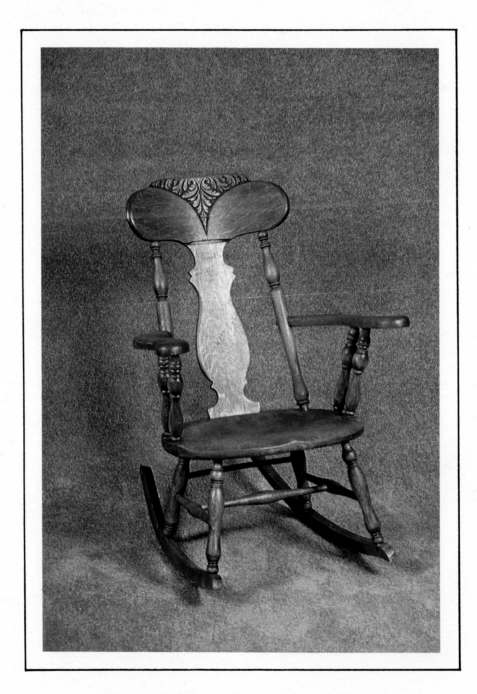

The sturdy oak pressback rocker above, breaks convention in that the back splays inward instead of the customary outward. The shapely center back splat shows the grain to advantage. Embossed pressing on the back appears to have some extra hand work.

a. This rocker has an upholstered shield in the American tradition. Oak.

b. Fancy turnings, pressings, applied machine-carved trim and bosses give a lively air to this decorative rocker. Oak.

c. Carved dolphin heads adorn the arms of the above rocker, with a veneered surface on the steam-bent back. Oak.

d. The pressed design on the veneered back, and the bulbous finials, are typical of the early 1900's. Oak.

Upholstered rocking chairs were sometimes called "the Farmer's friend". This title in the catalog copy would suggest that hard work deserved such a luxurious reward. Compared with today's soft easy chairs, the old-time luxury looks rather spartan.

(a) The back on this chair was machine carved over a pressing. The pattern resembles the "Old man winter" or "the North wind". Oak.

(b) A rocking chair built for comfort. Notice the bow-front or "swell" seat, the flat (rather than turned) back spindles, and the wide seat. Oak.

a. Rocker in quarter-sawn oak. Incised carved back, ladderback-style finials and turned back–posts soften the hard lines of mission-oak styling.

b. This chair has a pressed back and pressed upright posts which end in an almost "mouse-ear" design. The seat was made to be upholstered. Oak.

c. Applied molded composition trim, dark varnish and pseudo-Jacobean turnings, suggest an attempt at recreating the "antique" look. Oak.

d. Elegant swan heads are an unusual arm treatment on this classic rocker. Oak.

(a) Although the molded-veneer seat would suggest a later date, this oak pressback swing-platform rocker has a patent date of May 29, 1888 cast into the iron rocker swing supports. This invention, patent number 383805, was granted to George F. Hall of New York, and he assigned half the patent to Peter Lowentraut of Newark, N.J. However, the patent was only for the cast-iron hardware that the rocking chair rocked on. It is quite conceivable, therefore, that many manufacturers bought this rocker hardware and also made Hall-Lowentraut rocking chairs. Other patented platform rockers normally used springs or a combination of springs and swinging hardware. Another competing rocker of the same style was the McLean patent swing rocker.

a.

(b) Reclining platform rockers such as this were the fore-runners of the "Lazy-Boy" chair. A foot rest slides out from under the seat, and they were described in catalogs as being excellent for invalids. Today they are very suitable for television viewing. Some chairs of this type also swivel.

b.

The large platform spring rocker above has abundant turnings, superb finials and general stick-and-ball decoration. Notice the peculiar arm-support construction, often used on carpet rockers which are closely related. The platform rocks on heavy springs under the seat and the chair has two casters on the front to enable a housewife to move it. Platform rockers had their hey-day in the 1890's and seemed to be almost extinct in the catalogs of 1910. Distinctive pieces such as these are often used as accents in contemporary interiors.

a. A dentist's or barber's chair. It swivels and reclines, and the headrest adjusts. Oak.

b. Swivel oak pressback chair.

c. An office chair with an upholstered back and arms. Oak.

d. This piece reflects the *Art Nouveau* influence. Oak.

e. Bent-wood swivel chairs like this were used by early telephone switchboard operators. They also would have made good bar stools.

a. The child's rocker above has a pressed design on the back that resembles a pineapple skin. The posts have beehive finials.

b. Position of highchair below (d), lowered to become a rocking chair. Oak.

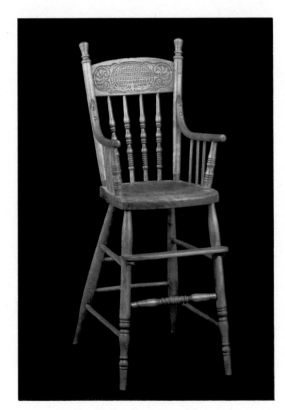

c. This type of highchair could have been ordered from the catalog with or without a food tray.

d. Children's adjustable highchairs were immensely popular. They could be changed into rocking chairs in an instant, and could also be pushed around on wheels like a carriage.

As people derived the benefits to be had from the 'New World' and living became easier, there was more time for things like education. Self-education was extremely popular and reading increased dramatically. Many houses boasted of having libraries so much that it became a status symbol to have even a modest library. Bookcases would have held the volumes and they took several forms, a few are pictured here:

(a) Stacking interlocking bookcases like this were modular units used primarily in offices. This set bears the label of Lyndstrom, Little Falls, New York. h. 48", w. 34", d. 13".
Each section is 11" high.

(b) John Danner Mfg. Co. of Canton, Ohio, patented this oak revolving bookcase which was very popular. It was featured in the Montgomery Ward catalog of 1894-5 where it was claimed two tiers would hold 32 volumes of "American Cyclopedia" or the three-tier version would hold 70-90 average volumes.
Oak. h. 49", w. 24", d. 24".

(c) Adjustable shelves and a curtain across the front to keep the books from getting dusty, made this a practical and inexpensive bookcase. This type was described in catalogs as a curtain library case or bookcase.

Today they have great potential as a practical and very decorative piece of furniture, curtained with period or modern fabric. Oak. h. 56", w. 32".

a.

b.

c.

a.

Two typical turn-of-the-century bookcase desks are illustrated here. They are small and functional, and well suited to small homes and apartments.

(a) Oak. h. 60", w. 30", d. 11".

(b) Bookcase desk signed Larkin.
Oak. h. 58", w. 28", d. 11".

Furniture manufactured by the Larkin Soap Manufacturing Co. of Buffalo N.Y. was given away as premiums to housewives who bought their soap. Premium catalogs issued twice a year, illustrated furniture for dining rooms, bedrooms, reception rooms, libraries and music rooms. In 1901, at the Pan-American Exposition, Larkin had their own building to display complete room settings, furnished with their premiums.

This well-constructed furniture was distributed throughout the United States, and today might be found in any area.

b.

a.

b. Detail of the marquetry decoration on the secretary desk (a). This medallion includes a beaver and a maple leaf, both Canadian symbols.

(a) This handsome secretary desk features marquetry detail that required the talents of a skilled craftsman. It was probably custom made.
Oak. h. 81", w. 41", d. 17".

Incised carving and a fretwork crest-rail decorate this impressive secretary desk. These details, and the use of carefully-selected woods, including a quarter-sawn drop-front, suggest the piece may have been custom made. All shelves in the cupboard section are adjustable.
h. 79", w. 38", d. 18".

a. An unusually light and graceful ladies' parlor desk. Oak. h. 42", w. 26", d. 17".

b. Fretwork cutouts indicate *Art Nouveau* influence on this drop-front desk. Oak. h. 43", w. 32", d. 16".

c. A sturdy letter desk. The inside contains several pigeon-holes.
Oak. h. 48", w. 33", d. 18".

d. A ladies' parlor desk.
Oak. h. 49", w. 38", d. 18".

The parlor desk above has applied machine-carved trim decorating the surface of the drop-front and the backboard. The two front legs would be classified as being French-style cabriole legs. It is unusual to have more than one drawer above the kneespace. This type of desk often has indications of scorching from a carelessly-placed oil lamp. Evidence of this is seen on the top right-hand lip above the drop-front.
Oak. h. 48", w. 29", d. 14".

In the past, desks made with a fold-out writing bed have been called drop-front, fall-front, sloping-front or slant-front. All these terms are correct, however, to save confusion, I have used *drop-front* to describe all desks of this type.

Desks are a symbol of authority as well as a useful item of furniture. In the past, the head of the house, the mistress of the house, and even the head butler would all have had position sufficient to warrant the use of a desk.

(a) This is a strongly-constructed desk which could have been used in a home office or by a student for homework. In the space on either side of the kneehole there are some rather impractical bookshelves. Pigeon holes inside the desk provide space for storing paperwork.
Oak. h. 44", w. 42", d. 14".

a.

(b) A pair of oil lamps placed on top of the cupboards would throw an even light on the desk surface. The hardware and the incised carvings on the doors are *Art Nouveau* in styling. The choice of well-grained quarter-sawn oak is excellent, and the large size suggests it was custom made.
h. 48", w. 58", d. 22".

b.

a. The strong plain lines of this mission-oak desk exude a strength and simplicity that was sought after during this period.
h. 46", w. 45", d. 19".

b. Jordan Marsh Co., Boston, Mass. put their label on this letter desk. It was probably made primarily for the large New England hotel trade.
Oak. h. 36", w. 36", d. 18".

c. A kneehole teacher's desk such a this would have been mounted on a small platform at the front of the class.
Oak. h. 35", w. 30", d. 26".

d. This drop-front desk has small cabriole legs and a fancy skirt that is incorporated into the bottom drawer. The writing bed is supported by two brass sliding brackets.
Oak. h. 40", w. 36", d. 20".

a.

(a) The oil-lamp bracket on this student's desk can also be inserted in the hole on the other side of the desk, thus school children doing their home studies could adapt the light to their needs. There is a paper slot, and holes for pencils and pens.
Oak. h. 33", w. 19", d. 15".

(b) Lyre-shaped ends lend a different look to this library table. Unusual shapes like this are popular today.
Oak. h. 28", w. 35", d. 24".

(c) The splayed legs of this library table, give it a certain flair.
Oak. h. 28", w. 37", d. 23".

Most library tables were of a useful size, although a number of them were more decorative than strong or functional. Library tables were used in reception or hall areas, in bedrooms for the use of students, and in the music room.

b.

c.

An open-mouthed lion, lion pulls and paw feet, adorn
this combination bookcase and writing desk. The trim
is all machine carved and applied.
Oak. h. 71", w. 38", d. 12".

Desks combined with long glass-enclosed bookcases were among the fanciest furniture fashions of the late-Victorian period. They were more costly and less practical than bookcase desks with a full-width desk area, but they did lend themselves to a greater range of flamboyant design and elaborate trim.

These bookcase desks are very popular today. In addition to their very decorative quality, they can be an excellent and appropriate display area for collections of the period, such as china, glass, miniature lamps, watches or jewelry. A kerosene or early electric lamp above the desk, and turn-of-the-century writing accessories would complement the piece.

a.

b.

(a) As on page 65, lions have their share of applied decoration on this piece. There is a knick-knack shelf in front of the fancy beveled mirror, upon which would sit a prized possession. Oak. h. 70", w. 36", d. 13".

(b) Die-cut embossed trim pieces are applied to the surface of this combination bookcase and writing desk. The catalog promotion claimed they were "nice enough for any house." Ash. h. 62", w. 38", d. 16".

a.

b.

(a) As a parlor desk, the cylinder roll-top type was considered slightly more desirable than a drop-front. This situation remains the same today.
Oak. h. 48", w. 29", d. 19".

(b) Six-drawer cylinder desk in oak.
h. 52", w. 32", d. 20".

(c) Roll-top desks are the choice of many today. Originally they were listed in the catalogs as office desks or curtain desks. The term roll-top appears to be a later name. Details such as size, "pigeon holes", drawer space, mail slots, the practicality of the writing bed and its covering, and the shape of the roll — whether it is an 'S' or a 'C' curve — all play a part in today's market price and desirability. The desk pictured here was ready for refinishing and would have originally had green cloth (baize) on the writing bed. Desks such as these are among the most sought-after pieces in today's furniture marketplace. Oak. Approx. h. 52", w. 60", d. 32".

c.

a.

It was customary for an affluent homeowner to have servants who would have been charged with the responsibility of assisting, at arrival and departure, with hats, coats, scarves, gloves, boots and umbrellas. These would have been stored, out of sight, in a closet.

Benches on this and the opposite page are typical of those used in large homes with spacious halls. Owners of such homes would be less likely to buy their furniture from a mail-order house, and therefore few examples of benches are found in the old catalogs.

Hall benches of the late 19th and early 20th century were usually either custom made or manufactured in small quantity. They are often found with elaborate ornamentation, carefully-selected woods and unusual design features.

(a) This bench has a striking stick-and-ball treatment on the back, combined with graceful lines. The style is quite unusual. Oak. h. 35", w 49", d. 16".

(b) Quarter-sawn oak is displayed to advantage on this mission-oak bench. The plain lines contrast dramatically with the other benches illustrated.

A horizontal oak-framed mirror, with or without hooks, was often placed above these benches.
Oak. h. 39", w. 36", d. 16".

b.

a. This ornate hall bench includes open-mouthed lions prominently displayed on the arms, a festooned applied trim, and an auspicious-looking urn in the center of the back. The seat lifts up for storage. Oak. h. 39", w. 48", d. 21".

b. Lions again! Impressive benches such as these were obviously designed to be showpieces. They were probably custom made. Oak. h. 45", w. 58", d. 20".

The hall bench with the mirror combination above are typical of those used in middle-class homes in the early 1900's. The plain lines also suggest the Edwardian period. Oak bench: h. 38", w. 42", d. 16". Mirror: 23" x 40".

a.

b.

A hall bench with a mirror, hat and coat racks or hooks, and an umbrella stand was a functional, fashionable feature of the average home. A wide range of styles, sizes and prices was advertised in the catalogs. There they were called hall stands, hall racks or hall trees, and the additional features were noted.

Hall furniture has always been considered very important, not only for any functional aspect that it provides, but because it quite literally is responsible for the first impression one receives when entering a home. The catalog copy writers appear to have been very much aware of this in their generous use of superlatives to describe every aspect that might impress visitors.

(a) This magnificent oak and ash hall stand with original oval beveled mirror and generous deep machine-carved embellishment has brass plated cast-iron hooks with lions in the center. The highly decorative nature of hall stands has placed them among the most sought-after pieces of catalog-era furniture. h. 84", w. 40", d. 16".

(b) A hall seat would have provided enough room for up to eight or more hats and coats. The weight of these often broke the cast-iron hooks. There was provision on this piece to have an umbrella stand, but passing fashion dictated its removal. The decoration on this piece is machine-carved and applied.
Oak. h. 83", w. 38", d. 17".

Lions carved on the armrests, and superb brass hooks with dolphins are notable aspects of this exceptionally fine hall stand. The seat lifts up and the carvings are applied. Oak. h. 80", w. 41", d. 20".

This hall stand finished in antique oak has pressed and incised carvings with applied machine-carved trim. There are umbrella hoops, but the drip trays are missing. The seat has doors under it.
Oak. h. 86", w. 45", d. 15".

a.

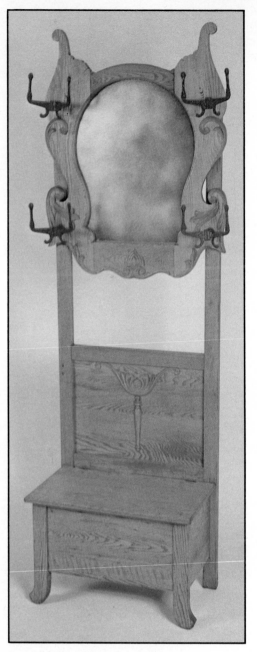

b.

(a) The outline or silhouette of the hall stands on this and the opposite page, illustrate the tremendous variation of form one might encounter today. Above is a sturdy example in oak. h. 78", w. 35", d. 15".

(b) There are at least two unusual features in this hall stand. One is the absence of arms, and the other is the odd shape of the top part. It appears to be upside down, and if such is the case, examination of the back revealed that the error was made long ago. Perhaps it was one of the pieces shipped "knocked down" for the shop or customer to assemble, or it might have been re-assembled after a move. Oak. h. 76", w. 29", d. 14".

a.

(a) There is always an element of surprise in each example that one encounters. It may be the way the fanciful trim is shaped and combined, or it may be in details such as unusual hooks or umbrella holders. Applied machine carvings decorate this piece. The umbrella holder at the side has a place for a drip tray. Over the years many of these holders broke off or were removed when umbrellas became less fashionable.
Oak. h. 78", w. 29", d. 15".

b.

(b) The wasp-waisted and flowing lines of this hall stand remind one of the women's fashions of the period. Oak. h. 80", w. 33", d. 16".

a.

b.

c.

Hall stands without seats would have been suitable for homes with a small entrance area or vestibule, or a narrow hallway. Some of these were anchored to the wall to prevent them from being tipped over by the weight of coats. The lighter ones were really intended for hats and umbrellas only, and were sometimes referred to as hat racks or umbrella stands. Coats would have been hung in a closet.

(a) Strong vertical lines dominate this stand with a particularly large capacity for umbrellas. It would likely have been anchored to the wall. Oak. h. 72", w. 22", d. 9".

(b) The small mirror on this hall stand is placed in a relatively high position. Brass plated hooks and the solid brass drip catcher are original. Oak. h. 74", w. 17", d. 11".

(c) Incised carvings adorn this hall stand with rather small delicate hooks. Elm. h. 77", w. 22", d. 17".

a.

c.

The pieces shown on this page would have originally been made primarily for office or commercial use. They were generally called hall trees or hat racks.

(a) Hat rack, or coat rack (it held both) that could have been used singly in homes, or in multiples for commercial or institutional use. In the home, hat racks like this would normally have been placed inside the rear or side door for use by the staff or family, and rarely placed in the reception area used for guests.

Hall trees like the mission-oak style (b) and the bent-wood version (c) were sometimes called costumers. Single-post hall trees are eagerly sought today as accents for offices and homes.

b.

Wind-up phonographs, today generically called Victrolas, were the start of the home entertainment business in America. Records bought at the local music store could play favorite songs over and over again. Sears Roebuck had their own phonograph factory and described the performance of their 'Truphonic' as follows: "until you actually hear it, you can never realize the startling perfection of the tone. No matter what kind of music — instrumental, or vocal, grand opera or jazz, a solo or a full orchestra, the Truphonic will play it for you just exactly like the original. You can hear each note with all the gradations in tone of every single instrument. Music flows forth from the Truphonic vibrant, eager, alive!"

Phonographs were available in a wide range of quality and price. It is therefore advisable to look for one that was a top-of-the-line model if you intend to use it. Old records in good condition and fiber or steel needles are scarce.

(a) Table model phonograph.

(b) "Nipper" listens to "His Masters Voice" on the label inside the lid of this Victrola. The volume was controlled by opening the doors just below the deck, and records were stored in the lower cabinet.

(c) The 'Lyre' symbol is a graceful form in the center of this sheet music stand. The label declared "It's a Hamilton" and "unbreakable base". Oak.

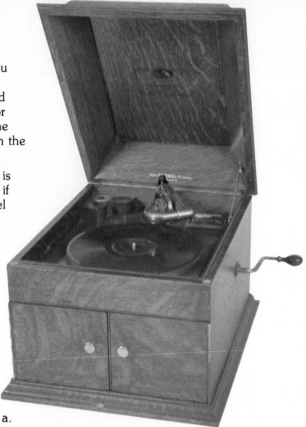

a.

b.

c.

This magnificent oak organ with lamp sconces, ornament shelves and
fretwork decoration, would probably have been used in a parlor or a church.
The organ was made by the Estey Organ Co., Brattleboro, Vt. Although
pump organs are readily available, they are seldom found in oak.

a.

(a) Servers were used in the dining room to store the silverware and tablecloths. The shelf below could have been for dessert trays or the tea set. Oak. h. 44", w. 38", d. 21".

(b) The seated lions supporting the shelf above the mirror, and the large lion-paw feet are features that place this piece in a very popular category today. Oak. h. 68", w. 52", d. 19".

(c) This sideboard has traces of Eastlake influence in its design. Elm. h. 51", w. 47", d. 18".

b.

c.

Superb quarter-sawn veneers face this sideboard. Note the three panels in the side, and embossed relief carvings. Generally low sideboards with mirrors were later than the highback-style mirrors. h. 60", w. 48", d. 19".

(a) The drop center on this sideboard must have been an attempt to combine a server with the sideboard. The silver drawer still exists. One cupboard to the side could be used to house the bar requirements. The two doors have an oak quarter-sawn veneer, and the rest is solid oak.   h. 55", w. 46", d. 21".

a.

(b) Whenever you see a top drawer bowed in this fashion you should check to see if it is a veneer. Veneers are desirable in sideboards or buffets, and this is a very attractive example.
Oak. h. 56", w. 49", d. 21".

b.

The high-backed sideboard above has leaded-glass china closets built into the sides. This style of sideboard, long overlooked, is becoming one of the most desirable pieces in oak furniture. Oak. h. 73", w. 48", d. 22".

This high-backed sideboard has an additional shelf under the mirror. Figurines and other ornaments were often well finished or decorated on the back, so that the reflected surface would be attractive when placed on a shelf or mantle, in front of a mirror. The trim is machine pressed and the double-paneled doors are unusual. Elm. h. 74", w. 46", d. 20".

Eastlake sideboards like this heralded the oak era. The unusual design suggests this one was probably custom made in a small workshop. Elm. h. 82", w. 52", d. 19".

before.

The "as found" condition of many pieces of oak, ash and elm furniture may include several layers of paint or a dark varnish stain. These "before and after" photographs illustrate the dramatic transformation that can occur with skillful refinishing. If the piece was originally stained or fumed, the color of the refinished piece will be affected. This sideboard shows some evidence of hand work. The fretwork supports and incised carvings on the door panels add to its appeal. Elm. h. 80", w. 48", d. 21".

after.

(a) This sideboard with large back and posts and knick-knack shelves surrounding a plain mirror, is typical of sideboards sold at the turn of the century. Applied machine carving adorns the top. Labeled, L. Morris, Bowmanville.
Elm. h. 72", w. 46", d. 20".

a.

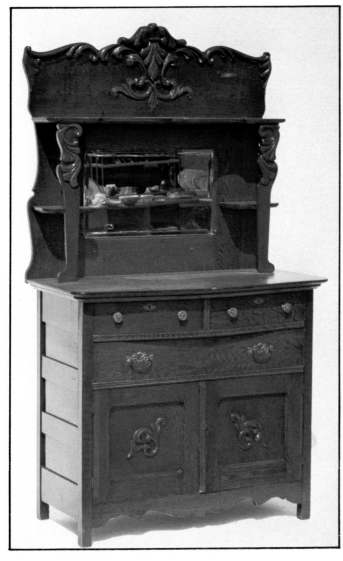

b.

(b) A magnificent high-backed oak sideboard, with an abundance of applied machine carving on the doors, uprights and top. The three drawers would have been used for silver and linen, and the cupboard was used for storing serving dishes and glassware. Often the silver drawer had a felt lining inside. During the 1890's, the mirror backs were tall and ornate. After World War I, the mirror proportions became long and narrow, and the frame plain in style.   h. 76", w. 44", d. 21".

The sideboard or buffet above has overall incised machine carving. Ornamentation and lines are derived from Eastlake. Elm. h. 80", w. 47", d. 22".

Heavy decoration has been applied to this high-backed buffet. The turned posts would have probably been incorporated to match the legs of a table in the set. Ash. h. 83", w. 52", d. 22".

This oak corner cupboard with lion-paw feet and mirrors on the back of the middle shelf, is an elegant example. Corner cupboards are rarely found in oak. h. 85".

Eastlake and country influence are combined in this two-piece kitchen cupboard, sometimes called a flat-to-the-wall or china closet. It has panels painted to imitate a burled-walnut veneer, and a pie shelf. Elm. h. 96", w. 49", d. 19".

Bent-glass china cabinets or closets are highly sought after today. Their popularity stems from their suitability as display cases for collections. The cabinet above has three bent-glass panels and lion-paw feet. The door molding is unusual. Oak. h. 64", w. 38", d. 17".

Quarter-sawn oak, lions atop the full-length columns, and lion-paw feet are features of this handsome bent-glass china cabinet. The key is used as a door pull.   h. 60", w. 36", d. 17".

a. Corner china closet — a type rarely found today. Oak. h. 59".

b. China cabinet with five adjustable shelves. Oak. h. 62", w. 30", d. 13".

c. Small elm china cabinet with a golden-oak finish.
Elm. h. 55", w. 30", d. 14".

d. China cabinet with sliding doors that can be locked.
Oak. h. 63", w. 35", d. 16".

The combination sideboard and china cabinet was often called a buffet. Pictured here are two similar examples.

a.

b.

(a) The leaded-glass door on this buffet is identical to that shown in (b). Both pieces also have bent-glass doors on the china cabinets. Quarter-sawn oak veneer is used on the cutlery drawers and the large linen drawer at the bottom with a modified swell front. The full-width shelf on the back could be used to display ornaments, or for serving. Above and below it are two narrow beveled mirrors.
h. 60", w. 42", d. 17".

(b) Although the backs and legs differ, these two buffets have sufficient similarities to suggest they were made by the same manufacturer.
h. 56", w. 42", d. 17".

A china cabinet and sideboard combination. The cabinet has a
full-length bent-glass door. Applied machine carvings and
lion-paw feet enhance this piece.
Oak. h. 75", w. 50", d. 17".

a.

(a) In 1890, George Hunzinger of New York, N.Y. obtained an invention patent for a "combination chair and table". The main features of his claim related to the appearance and effect when the chairs were pushed under the table. They provided a shelf under the table top, and the design of the chair backs gave the appearance of an apron under the table. The grouping above has been referred to as a "games table set" or as an "ice cream set". There is a small suspended shelf under the table top. The patent date, August 5, 1890, is embossed on a metal plate on the top of a leg. Oak. h. 28", w. 30", d. 30".

(b) The top of this table may be rotated to reveal pockets that would hold chips. Brass beading trims the top.
Oak. h. 35", w. 31", d. 31".

b.

a.

b.

c.

Parlor tables were made in almost every conceivable shape. Their uses included end tables, plant stands, book tables and smokers' tables. Today they are used to hold television sets, stereo equipment, telephones and the inevitable plant. Tables of this vintage were generally more stylish than strong. Some are flamboyant, and some have flagrantly taken features from several periods and put them together in ways that may be confusing, annoying or enjoyable!

(a) A drop-leaf end table with unusually thin cabriole legs, and carved ball-and-claw feet. Oak. h. 31", w. 17", d. 18".

(b) This small parlor table with tapered legs is a good example of the work of the Paines Furniture Mfg. of Boston, Mass. Oak. h. 26", w. 16", d. 16".

(c) A parlor table also by Paines of Boston. Triangular pieces of quarter-sawn oak veneer create a striking pattern. Oak. h. 28", w. 24", d. 24".

a.

Tables like the ones shown on this page are used by cross-country haulers to fill empty spaces in larger pieces of furniture. They are usually dismantled for shipping.

(a) Parlor tables like this, with large glass-ball and brass-claw feet, are scarce today. They command a considerably higher price than similar tables with smaller feet.
Oak. h. 29", w. 28", d. 28".

(b) A plain parlor table with a shelf below to add strength. Almost every house during the oak era had one or more parlor tables.
Oak. h. 30", w. 20", d. 20".

b.

c.

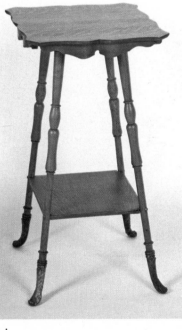

d.

(c) Parlor table with small glass-ball and cast-iron-claw feet. Oak. h. 28", w. 21", d. 21".

(d) Petite dolphin feet and a fancy apron grace this oak table. h. 28", w. 17", d. 17".

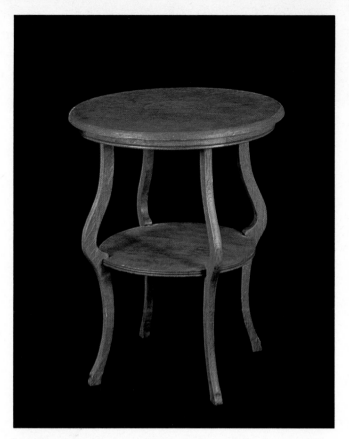

a. Drop-leaf parlor table with drawer.
Elm. h. 30", w. 35", d. 24".

b. Small round parlor table with bookshelf
below. Oak.

c. Round parlor table. Oak. h. 30", 24" dia.

d. Square parlor table with machine pressings on
the apron. Oak. h. 29", w. 27", d. 27".

(a) A small "stick-and-ball" jardinier stand. Oak.

(b) Three-legged table with a cloverleaf top. This type of table was made in many different woods, with many variations in design. They ranged from sophisticated styles to simple country tables reminiscent of early candle stands.

(c) The scrolls, pad feet and unusual design suggest that this table is one of a kind, possibly made by a skilled amateur. On the middle shelf is a bowl-like depression.
Oak. h. 33", w. 12", d. 12".

(d) This small square end table was probably used as a jardinier stand.
Oak. h. 29", w. 12", d. 12".

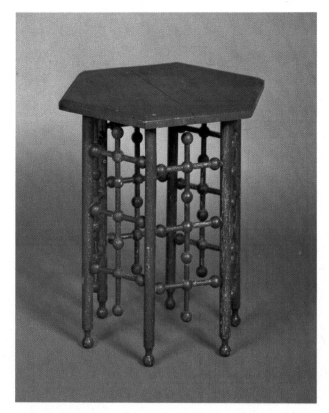

a.

b.

c.

d.

Rectangular tables, such as the ones illustrated here, were used as parlor tables. They were often placed in front of a window to hold a decorative "gone-with-the-wind" type oil lamp. The diversity of the oak era is apparent in these tables that incorporate styles from many periods.

a.

(a) An Oriental influence is shown in this parlor table with a bevel-edge top, and a shelf below for books or periodicals.
Elm. h. 29", w. 34", d. 22".

(b) Pretty, neat, handsome and fancy were all adjectives used in the catalogs to describe parlor tables. The incised carvings and gingerbread apron would most likely have been referred to as "fancy".
Elm. h. 29", w. 32", d. 23".

b.

a.

b.

(a) A rectangular bedroom table.
Oak. h. 28", w. 24", d. 17".

(b) Features of this Eastlake parlor table include incised carving, and an unusual turned cross-stretcher, that adds extra strength.
Elm. h. 29", w. 32", d. 22".

(c) An Oriental influence sometimes referred to as "Japanese Revival" is apparent in this parlor table.   h. 29", w. 24", d. 24".

c.

a. Base detail of a plain round oak pedestal or pillar extension table. Catalogs refer to this base, and that of (b) as a 'Colonial' foot. Diameter of the top is 52".

b. A rather plain, smaller (42" diameter), round oak table in a basic style. Reproductions of this style are available, and are occasionally difficult to identify unless you check the underside and the pedestal pillar inside. A reproduction rarely has any darkening of the wood. This is sometimes called "air burn" or "patina".

c. A good 42" round oak table with attractive lion-paw feet. These feet were often described as smooth cut hand carved. Round oak pedestal tables were featured in catalogs in the early 1900's.

d. This pedestal has 'swell' sides covered with a quarter-sawn veneer. The lion-paw feet support a platform that provides a firm base for the 45" diameter top. This table had two leaves.

e. Base detail of a round table showing roaring lions and paw feet. Today there would be several hundred dollars difference between this table and the example (c) with just the paws. Diameter of the top is 45".

a. This plain 42" round oak table with a square pedestal pillar is often sold to complement mission-style furniture. This table and the one on the right have 'Colonial' bases similar to (a) and (b) on the opposite page.

b. The popularity of round tables ensures a brisk market for all styles, however, the price difference between the top and the bottom of the scale may be many hundreds of dollars.

c. The center pillar of this 45" diameter oak pedestal table does not divide for insertion of leaves, instead the legs with lion-paw feet, pull away from the pillar when the top is divided and extended. The table then becomes a five-leg table. The 1908 Sears Roebuck Co. catalog illustrated a table similar to this one and described the feet as "lions-claw". The extended sizes for sale included a 6', 8', 10' and a massive 12' table.

Fancy oak rectangular extension tables with lion-paw feet, such as this heavily-carved example, have always been popular, and are now becoming scarce. Note the bowed stretchers between the end legs which allow ample leg room for diners. The center legs will support many leaves.   h. 29", w. 50", d. 50".

a.

The catalog-promotion descriptions of these tables made mention of some interesting points. "The top has a full boxed rim beautifully shaped with perfectly framed and mitred corners." Several factories, in different areas, were often charged with the responsibility of supplying the identical table for the catalogs. Sears Roebuck, for instance, shipped the quarter-sawn oak orders in some cases from factories in the East or Midwest, and the plain-sawn oak orders from Indiana. It is also interesting to note that it was a general practice for manufacturers not to finish the leaves as well as the main table top because "that when in use they are covered by the tablecloth".

Extension tables like the examples on this page would have had up to six leaves.

(a) Notice the 'quarter-sawn' appearance of the turned legs. The legs were detachable for shipping and were usually packed inside the top of the table. The legs frequently, as in this case, went askew. The center leg would give support for the extra leaves when the table was extended. In some instances where the leaves are missing, and the fifth center leg is no longer necessary, it is removed, inverted, mounted on a base and made into an electric lamp.
Oak. h. 30", w. 42", d. 42".

(b) These dining tables were very common in America during the oak era. A few years ago they were sitting unwanted in stores, but recently have come into their own, and now are becoming more difficult to locate. This table has six legs.
Oak. h. 29", w. 40", d. 40".

b.

a.   A similar drop-leaf extension table was described in the 1897 Sears Roebuck catalog as ". . . an old time favorite and never goes out of date, nor does it lose any of its desirable features", and also "can be taken apart and shipped knocked down, thus saving very largely in the freight rate." This one is ash and measures 44" x 52".

b. The space-saving aspect of drop-leaf tables accounts for their popularity among apartment dwellers. This handsome and unusual one has large D-shaped leaves, and modified lion-paw feet. Oak. h. 29", w. 42", d. 59".

Kitchen cabinets provided work space and storage for food and equipment. Some were quite decorative, and some contained more features than others. Among these were provision for calendars, notes and recipe books, built-in shopping reminders, flour sifters, bake or cutting boards, metal-lined bread drawers, an extension work surface, divided cutlery drawers, cupboards that were equipped with racks for spices, etc., and shelves for storage of food, dishes and utensils.

a.

Kitchen cabinets are frequently called "Hoosier" cabinets or cupboards due to their manufacture and popularity in Indiana, the Hoosier State.

(a) This kitchen cabinet has leaded-glass doors, a pull-out bakeboard, a metal-lined bread drawer and many cupboards for storage. Elm. h. 75", w. 44", d. 27".

(b) Features of this kitchen cabinet include a rollup wooden curtain, caramel-slag glass windows and a vitreous enamel pull-out counter-top. Oak. h. 70", w. 48", d. 27".

b.

There are some who may not be aware of the many differences between living with today's refrigerator and its predecessor the ice box. Ice was delivered on a regular basis all year round to every house possessing one of these 'modern devices'.

Most ice boxes had a compartment at the top for a large block of ice. A drainage pipe ran from this compartment to a tray under the ice box. It was always a tricky maneuver to remove an almost-full tray and empty it into the kitchen sink without spilling some water on the floor. This, however, was not as unfortunate a circumstance as forgetting to empty the tray and having the kitchen floor flooded (particularly if it was *your* job to empty it).

a.

b.

In operation, air surrounding the block of ice in the upper compartment was cooled and flowed down to the food compartment below. As the air warmed up, it rose again to be "purified and cooled" once more. Ice was heralded as "the greatest purifier known to modern science". Odorless charcoal was used as an insulation material. To use an ice box you would need ice tongs for moving the ice, ice chippers, ice picks, ice chisels and shaves, and if you had children, you would have to have an ice shredder to make ice balls to which were added juices and flavors as in "sno cones" today. Chipped ice was also used in ice cream freezers for family treats. The attraction to the gourmet was evident in the catalog promotion which mentioned shaving ice for use in fruits, drinks, oysters on-the-half-shell, olives, celery, iced tea, sliced tomatoes, etc.

(a) A four-door oak ice box or refrigerator which would have been used in a large household. h. 49", w. 34", d. 19".

(b) This 'Chautauqua' model ice box was made by the Larkin Co. of Buffalo, N.Y. Today most ice boxes are bought to house stereo or bar equipment. Oak. h. 43", w. 25", d. 18".

(a) The scalloped skirt adds interest to an otherwise plain ice box. It also has a lift lid on the ice compartment and brass hardware.
Ash. h. 42", w. 31", d. 21".

a.

b. Incised carvings and excellent brass hardware make this 'Chicago' brand ice box or refrigerator highly desirable today.
Elm. h. 40", w. 28", d. 18".

c. Ice chests are often used today as wine coolers. They differed from ice boxes in that the block of ice was placed in the same compartment as the food and the air did not circulate.
Ash. h. 28", w. 34", d. 22".

What-nots, often called *étagères,* were very popular during the Victorian period. They were used to display an assortment of china, glass and porcelain that might include figurines, vases and paperweights, and also ornaments, souvenirs, photographs and other memorabilia. Today they are used to display collections of these articles.

The design of what-nots corresponded with the objects they displayed. They were fussy, usually fragile, and rarely made in oak. They were seldom sold through catalogs, perhaps because their fragile construction created shipping problems.

The exceptional example opposite would be classed as "Japanese revival" with its oriental fretwork and shape reminiscent of a pagoda. The wood is oak, and the finish is antique oak. h. 45", w. 26", d. 14".

Woods

In North America today the identification of oak is a difficult task even for an expert. It remains to be said that a large percentage of wooden furniture sold or classified as "oak" is categorically not oak, however, the term *oak furniture* is used generically. The tendency to hear only what one wants to hear applies, and when dealers hear the cry for "oak", it means any coarse-grained hardwood. Several times during my travels I spotted elm, ash or chestnut only to be told firmly, in no uncertain terms, that it was oak. This self deception the market practises stems from the final retail market ignorance of the subject, and really so long as the customer is happy, then people such as myself should not be making waves or even ripples in the pond — or should we? Whether we can clarify the identification confusion over the years remains to be seen. Some of the old catalogs advertising the type of furniture shown in this book boasted "fine Kentucky white oak" and "Indiana quarter-sawed oak" as their primary sources of woods, but most manufacturers bought wood from wherever they could. Indications of this are the "kiln-dried Northern hardwood" description which covers a multitude of true identities. Northern hardwood could quite conceivably be almost any of the following coarse-grained woods: white ash, elm, chestnut, hickory, chestnut oak, red oak, white oak, pin oak, black oak, scarlet oak, bur oak, willow oak, and many species of hybrid oak-type trees.

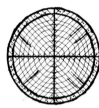 

Quarter-sawn oak.

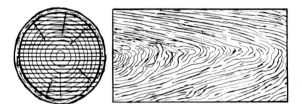

Plain-sawn oak.

What the manufacturers or sellers knew of the woods themselves is not altogether clear. Sears Roebuck & Co. frequently used the term "made from selected material". In their own words, for example, a garden bench was listed as being made of "select kiln-dried wood and is finished in either regular, green or antique oak". Thus an unsuspecting customer may have been led to believe that his bench would be made of solid oak.

Having challenged both past and present dealers with the myths and mysteries of oak identification, I can only suggest that if one really wishes to know the truth, scientific testing with a microscope is the best method of identification.

If you are not satisfied with the description or identification of your wood, by all means satisfy your curiosity and take a small sliver of wood exposing the end grain from an inside back leg where the chip will not be missed, then find out from your local museum or dealer where they have their wood samples analyzed. This done, put numbers or some identification mark on the sliver, put it into a plastic sample bag, and send it to the laboratory — then wait. The results are often interesting and exciting. It is predictable that more collectors and dealers will resort to wood analysis in the future.

As we traveled about the country, it would have obviously been unmannerly to have collected specimens from pieces not in our possession, so for the purpose of this book, I generally used an educated guess based on verbal information and visual identification.

Quarter-sawn Oak

Large amounts of furniture were made from quarter-sawn (or sawed) oak. As the name implies, this was a special cut of oak in which the logs were sawn into quarters lengthwise to expose the grain rays running from the heart to the bark. This was a more expensive process because it necessitated more handling, entailed more loss than conventional cutting and required larger logs. There were, however, advantages other than surface beauty in that quarter-sawn oak shrinks less in width and warps less than plain-sawn lumber, thus making it more desirable for use in furniture.

The illustration shows both the quarter-sawn and the plain-sawn methods. Note the pronounced swirling pattern of the quarter-sawn oak as opposed to the straight grain of the plain-sawn oak.

Finishes

Finishes to protect the oak from the ravages of wear and tear were almost as many as there were manufacturers.

Most of the factories had their own secret formulas for producing a desirable end product. To some people, furniture finishing was regarded as an art in itself and they went to great lengths to obtain what they considered to be a desirable finish. It was felt that new white oak had to be aged and given exposure to impart a depth and mellowness to the finish. However, natural aging of the wood for the many years necessary was out of the question to men in a hurry. After much experimentation, an enterprising person found out towards the end of the century that if one exposed raw oak wood to the fumes of ammonia, it would age and darken the wood in double-quick time.

Fumed Oak

The method of making 'fumed' oak was as follows: after the furniture was assembled, it was rubbed all over with water to open up the pores and the grain. The pieces were then placed in oven-like air-tight containers into which were placed basins full of a strong ammonia solution. The curing time was usually about forty-eight hours, give or take some, depending on the depth of color required. After the fuming, the wood was sanded again to remove all the raised grain fibers. Then the final lacquer finish was applied.

Anyone who has tried in recent times to remove this 'stain' will have had a difficult time of it. Even many hours of sanding will not budge the stubborn color impregnated deep into the wood by 'fuming'.

Golden Oak

Possibly the most sought after of the original oak finishes, golden oak is certainly the most desired color today. Generally it was produced by putting a hard orange shellac finish, with the possible addition of some yellow ochre pigments, over the whiteness of the oak.

Weathered Oak

This was a delicate gray finish with a silvery sheen such as would be produced by the effects of sun and wind. It was also achieved by fuming, but with the addition of driftwood type stains.

Antique Oak

Catalogs frequently sold pieces of furniture in the antique oak finish. Some manufacturers used stains to effect a nutty brown hue usually associated with 'air burn' which is caused by long-term exposure to ultra-violet sun rays. Other manufacturers used the terminology to describe a shading technique which was used around highlighted areas, and was usually applied by spray finishing.

These four finishes and colors were generally used for most catalog furniture, but there was also a finish alluded to as 'piano polished' which must have been a high-gloss finish to simulate 'French polishing'.

A fake oak finish can be confusing to the unsuspecting buyer. When oak lumber ran out and became too expensive, other hard woods were printed with black ink, then colored an oak brown to simulate oak grain. The easiest way to spot this occurrence today is to check the back face of the wood in the furniture and if it is different from the grain on the face surface, then be warned.

Influences

American oak furniture was subject to many influences that resulted in a variety of designs and finishes. Affluence, technology, rapid change, marketing, travel and communication were all factors that motivated Victorian eclecticism. Certain designs, manufacturers and schools had a distinct effect on furniture styles during the Victorian era and the early 1900's. Some of the better known are listed below.

Morris

William Morris (1834-1896) of England led a reform group advocating the adoption of a return to "good taste". He felt that good design could only come back by way of honest hard labor, a return to the medieval way of life and hand methods of making furniture. In part, his rebellion was against the machinery of the industrial revolution and partly against Victorian styles. His own furniture did not sell well in England, but his plain and simple designs sowed the seeds for the 'Arts and Crafts' movement which flourished from 1882 until World War I in 1914.

Eastlake

Charles Locke Eastlake (1836-1906) of England, wrote a book titled *Hints on Household Taste* printed first in England in 1868 and in America in 1872, which proved to be immensely popular. Although he advocated simple, honest design, his philosophies and principles were misconstrued and distorted to the extent that furnishings referred to as 'Eastlake' bore little resemblance to his ideas.

American Eastlake is hard to define, nonetheless, 'Eastlake' may be considered a general style which embodies stylized design, square shapes and much trim of a geometric nature. Vertical turnings and the use of incised carving rather than applied trim were essential to the 'Eastlake' look.

Eastlake and Morris subscribed to parallel philosphies about the return to medieval ways and although Eastlake's styles were more elaborate than those of Morris, they both in turn left their mark on the American 'Arts and Crafts' movement.

Thonet

Michael Thonet (1796-1871) of the Prussian Thonet brothers developed bent-wood chairs in their Vienna, Austria factory that could be shipped "knocked down". The Thonet family was ahead of its time and first manufactured their chairs after being granted patents in 1841 for France, England and Belgium. In 1851 at London's Crystal Palace, he was sufficiently entrenched as an exporter to warrant a display in the Great Exhibition. The Thonets had warehouses in New York and Chicago and exerted a strong influence on American furniture.

Stickley

Out of a typical furniture manufacturing concern came Gustav Stickley. With his brothers and partners he produced much furniture at Syracuse, N.Y. from the early 1880's until 1898 when he traveled to England and other parts of Europe. He returned with a new outlook and thus a radical new concept in American furniture was born. He introduced his new form to America at the 1900 Grand Rapids, Michigan, Furniture Exposition, where he received instant acclaim.

Gustav Stickley sent his messages about furniture out to his market by means of a well-planned and written "Craftsman" catalog which he painstakingly produced annually from 1901-1913. He bypassed the catalog mail-order houses and directly approached the public himself. His catalogs were not just a sales tool but obvious propaganda forums where his philosophies, teachings and ideas relating to his interpretation of the 'Arts and Crafts' movement were expounded convincingly. He steadfastly believed that the selection of furniture and the placing of it in the home environment exerted strong moral influences on the people living with it. Thus furniture was not just a practical or esthetic necessity, it was a moral imperative to families of the time to create a 'proper' environment.

His willingness to sell his designs to home-crafters and supply them with the patterns and hardware showed his missionary belief that the availability of his style influences should not be solely for people who could buy his furniture. This was in keeping with the 'Arts and Crafts' philosophy of finding joy in work and self reliance.

Leopold and J. George Stickley, brothers of the famous Gustav, followed closely in his footsteps in the furniture they produced.

Larkin

The Larkin Soap Manufacturing Company was an immensely successful premium operation. At the height of their popularity they mailed one-and-a-half million catalogs, twice a year. Their primary interest was to sell soap but the business of giving gifts to customers in return for soap orders founded a huge empire of furniture manufacturing in Buffalo, N.Y.

Started as the John D. Larkin Company in 1875, it progressed through slight name changes and became the Larkin Soap Manufacturing Company in 1892. John Larkin (1845-1926) was fortunate to have as a member of his family and firm, Elbert Hubbard, who was his brother-in-law. Hubbard's marketing expertise and skill at writing made the "Larkin Club" important to the multitudes of housewives who bought soap on the installment plan to obtain the highly desirable furnishings from the catalogs.

Hubbard left Larkin in 1893 and became an influential style trend setter in his own right.

Hubbard

At the age of 35, Elbert Hubbard (1856-1915) decided to alter the course of his life and left his successful career with Larkin to set up his own colony of 'Arts and Crafts' movement supporters at East Aurora, N.Y. Hubbard named the commune the 'Roycrofters'. He developed ideas similar to Stickley after a trip to England and encounters with the Morris philosophies. The Roycrofters influenced furniture, printing, bookbinding and metalwork until Hubbard was tragically killed in the 1915 sinking of the 'Lusitania'.

Limbert

The Limbert Brothers of Grand Rapids, Michigan, were the Midwest's answer to the New York 'Arts and Crafts' movement.'

Greene

The Greene Brothers of California also contributed, although far removed from the center of the market. They were known for their adaptations of the Oriental influence.

Mission Oak

Mission-oak furniture was described thusly in a 1908 Sears Roebuck catalog:
"This style of furniture is no longer an experiment but after the test of years is now one of the most popular styles on the market

for all who appreciate beauty and simplicity of design combined with strength and comfort. It derives its name from the original pieces found in an old Spanish Mission in Southern California, and has been approved and accepted by the Arts and Crafts Societies of the United States and England. Prominent architects throughout the country recommend and specify this style and finish".

The Sears explanation is excellent, and I can only add that according to Robert Bishop, the American Mission-style probably started in 1894 at the Second Jerusalem Church of San Francisco where the congregation made their own furniture.

Mission-style furniture originally was smoked but the fumed–oak finish became more popular and Gustav Stickley was one of its greatest and most respected manufacturers.

L'Art Nouveau

European schools of design played a role in American Art Nouveau furniture. The French equivalent to the 'Arts and Crafts' movement was embodied in *L'Art Nouveau* which used forms found in nature such as flowers and leaf lines.

Henri Van de Velde (1863-1957) who emerged as the genius of *L'Art Nouveau* at the 1894 Brussels Exhibition, and subsequent exhibitions in Paris in 1895 and Dresden in 1897 established the style. By 1900 it was the sensation of Europe. His work and forms were accepted in France, Austria, Belgium, and Germany predominantly, and in 1902 he was invited to open the *Bauhaus School* at Weimar, Germany.

In Austria, the movement was known as *the Secession*. There they added the English 'Arts and Crafts' movement to their philosophies and in 1903 opened the *Wiener Werkstätte* in Vienna.

Expositions

Although the written word established the groundwork for style change and acceptability, it remained for the furniture to be seen by the public to really gain acceptance. Exhibitions, sometimes called expositions, provided international influence.

Some of the landmark expositions were: The Chicago Exposition of 1893 where the return to classicism was inspired; The Paris Exposition of 1900 which swung the acceptance of 'Art Nouveau'; The Grand Rapids, Michigan, Furniture Exposition of 1900 where the public acceptance of Mission styling was launched.

Exhibitions were an ongoing occurrence and it is difficult to pin down exact traces of influence on American oak furniture to many of them.

Buyers Guidelines

Experience in the marketplace will hone your intuition, and no amount of reading will give you this exposure.

To start a neophyte buyer on the way, there are several hints capsuled here which may help.

In order to see through paint, you do not need X-ray eyes, just a small penknife to do a test scrape to check the grain. However, DO NOT choose a visible surface to scrape; choose a back leg or an inside drawer-front *and please ask permission*. When you get better acquainted with the woods, you may try "finger tapping" the wood just as a medical doctor checks a patient. Different woods have varying sounds and you can tell oak from pine after a little practice, but telling other woods apart can be quite difficult.

A painted piece may have a relatively inexpensive price tag, but remember there may be reasons for this. Refinishing is hard work, and under the paint you quite often have hidden water rings or cigarette burns. These are your unknown factors and may not be worth the risk. If the piece has been varnished, it may be possible to spot a hidden blemish by looking closely at the surface.

Check the bottoms of the legs on pieces for "basement rot" which is a common cause of feet wasting away to dust. It is caused by a piece sitting on a damp floor for too long. Check out the piece for evidence of wood-borers; small holes will be the sign.

Some oak repairs are costly to have done when there are splits involved or if there is a door or drawer missing from a piece. Nonetheless you should learn as early as possible which repairs are regularly expected to be simple and can be tackled by an amateur, versus the average complex professional basket-case.

New collectors are often hesitant to trust dealers after hearing all kinds of horror stories, but when you go out hunting you will find that often your best source of knowledge will be your dealer. Bear in mind also that the antique business is quite competitive and has its own built-in supply and demand system for checking market excesses of quantity or price. If there is too much of something at too high a price, it just won't sell and dealers are constantly aware of the current market situations. Remember dealers can only remain in operation if they sell and turn over their stock like any other retail business.

When assessing a purchase price, take into consideration that you will pay accordingly for: quality, condition, potential investment value, and whether it is an unusual or rare piece. Do not hesitate to ask questions if you're unsure about any of the qualifications.

Bibliography

Selected

Altman, Seymour and Violet. *The Book of Buffalo Pottery.* New York: Bonanza Books, 1967.

Aronson, Joseph. *The Encyclopedia of Furniture.* New York: Crown Publishers, Inc., 1938.

Boger, Louise Ade and H. Batterson. *The Dictionary of Antiques and the Decorative Arts.* New York: Charles Scribner's Sons, 1957.

Bishop, Robert. *Centuries and Styles of the American Chair, 1640-1970.* New York: E. P. Dutton & Co. Inc., 1972.

_____ *Guide to American Antique Furniture.* New York: Galahad Books, 1973.

Butler, Joseph T. *American Furniture.* London: Triune Books, 1973.

Eastlake, Charles L. *Hints on Household Taste.* New York: Dover Publications. Reprint of the 1872 book, 1969.

Edlin, Herbert L. *What Wood is That?* New York: Viking Press, 1969.

Gaines, Edith and Jenkins, Dorothy H. *The Woman's Day Dictionary of Antique Furniture.* New York: Hawthorn Books, 1974.

Grotz, George. *The Furniture Doctor.* New York: Doubleday & Co., 1962.

Hill, Conover. *Value Guide to Antique Oak Furniture.* Paducah, Kentucky: Collector Books, 1972.

Honour, Hugh. *Cabinet Makers and Furniture Designers.* New York: Hamlyn Publishing Group Ltd., 1972.

Ormsbee, Thomas H. *Field Guide to American Victorian Furniture.* New York: Bonanza Books, 1952.

Sloane, Eric. *A Reverence for Wood.* New York: Funk & Wagnalls, 1965.

Stickley, Gustav. *Craftsman Furniture Catalogs.* New York: Dover Reprint, 1979.

Wise, Herbert. *Made with Oak.* New York: Links Books, 1975.

Numerous catalog reprints of the Department Stores Mail Order Systems.

Some of the more useful ones are:

Montgomery Ward & Co. 1894 & 1895 Northfield, Illinois: Gun Digest, 1970.

Sears Roebuck, 1897 New York: Chelsea House Publishers, 1968.

Sears Roebuck Fall, 1900 Northfield, Illinois: Digest Books Inc., 1970.

Sears Roebuck, 1908 Northfield, Illinois: Digest Books Inc., 1971.

The T. Eaton Co., 1901 Toronto: The Musson Book Co., 1970.

Catalog of *The Great Exhibition of London 1851.* New York: Crown Publishers. Reprinted 1970.

General

Fales, Dean A. Jr. *American Painted Furniture 1660-1880.* New York: E. P. Dutton and Co. Inc., 1979.

Hornung, Clarence P. *Treasury of American Design,* Two Volumes in One. New York: Harry N. Abrams, Inc.

Kovel, Ralph and Terry. *American Country Furniture 1780-1875.* New York: Crown Publishers, Inc., 1965.

Miller, Edgar G. Jr. *American Antique Furniture.* Two Volumes. New York: Dover Reprint of the 1937 original.

Nutting, Wallace. *The Furniture Treasury, Volumes I and II.* New York: The MacMillan Company, 1928.

Pain, Howard. *The Heritage of Country Furniture.* Toronto: Van Nostrand Reinhold Ltd., 1978.

Index

Author

Peter Blundell, with his wife Marian, operate an antique shop in the Village of Schomberg, near Toronto, Ontario. Born and educated in England, his early interests ranged from "white elephant sales" to visiting the great museums and galleries. After studying retail distribution at London City and Guilds, he was employed on Savile Row. He has traveled extensively in Europe, and overland across the American Continent several times. He lived on the West Coast and in Quebec before settling in the Toronto area.

Peter has worked at flea markets and antique shows, as a 'picker' and as a 'hauler' and understands the everyday workings of the antique trade.

Designer

Catherine Thuro is the author and designer of OIL LAMPS, *The Kerosene Era in North America* and PRIMITIVES & FOLK ART, *our handmade heritage*.

She undertook the organization and production of this book at the request of the publisher and enlisted the experience and enthusiasm of antiques dealer, Peter Blundell.

THE MARKETPLACE GUIDE TO

OAK FURNITURE
Styles & Values

PETER S. BLUNDELL

Oak, elm and ash furniture has seen a phenomenal rise in popularity during the last decade. This interest has resulted in values that reflect the demand for certain pieces, i.e. sideboards versus dressers, and the demand for certain details such as style, color or trim.

In addition to this there are marked regional differences in price. Geographically speaking, values grow as pieces move inland from the Eastern Seaboard to the Midwest, and then soar upwards to peak near the Western shores. Prices in this supplement are expressed in U.S. currency, and are those that one might expect to encounter in the Eastern States.

With the above considerations taken into account, prices for the examples in this book may be used as a yardstick to measure prospective purchases.

The Marketplace Guide to Oak Furniture contains much information which will develop an understanding of the marketplace. The checklist below is a reminder of the salient points to consider.

- Repairs or restoration that have been made, or are required.
- Original finish and its condition, or the quality and condition of refinished wood.
- Original hardware or mirrors.
- Condition of the interior. Both cleanliness and completeness are to be considered.
- Condition of caning or upholstery, and whether it is original or replaced.
- Solid and selected woods.
- Signed or labeled.

The majority of pieces illustrated were mass produced, and the same or similar examples may be found today.

COLLECTOR BOOKS   Box 3009   Paducah, Kentucky 42001

All prices are for restored and refinished items or items with original finish in good condition.

BEDROOM FURNITURE

Page 17 }
Page 18 } 3 piece set . . . . . . $8,500 — 9,000

Page 19
    (a) . . . . $495 — 535
    (b) . . . . $495 — 535
Page 20
    (a) . . . . $525 — 575
    (b) . . . . $345 — 375
Page 21 . . . . $500 — 550
Page 22
    (a) . . . . $325 — 350
    (b) . . . . $245 — 265
    (c) . . . . $385 — 400
    (d) . . . . $385 — 400
Page 23
    (a) . . . . $400 — 435
    (b) . . . . $400 — 435
Page 24
    (a) . . . . $465 — 495
    (b) . . . . $465 — 495
Page 25
    (a) . . . . $365 — 385
    (b) . . . . $365 — 385
    (c) . . . . $345 — 365
    (d) . . . . $385 — 400
Page 26 . . . . $385 — 400
Page 27 . . . . $345 — 365
Page 28 . . . . $475 — 500
Page 29
    (a) . . . . $325 — 345
    (b) . . . . $525 — 550
    (c) . . . . $800 — 850
Page 30
    (a) . . . . $235 — 265
    (b) . . . . $225 — 240
Page 31 . . . . $285 — 295
Page 32 . . . . $265 — 295
Page 33 . . . . $395 — 425
Page 34
    (a) . . . . $245 — 265
    (b) . . . . $395 — 425
    (c) . . . . $375 — 395
Page 35 . . . . $475 — 500
Page 36
    (a) . . . . $575 — 600
    (b) . . . . $385 — 400
    (c) . . . . $295 — 325
Page 37 . . . . $550 — 595

CHAIRS

Page 38 . . . . $275 — 300
Page 39
    (a) . . . . $115 — 135
    (b) . . . . $225 — 250
Page 40 . . . . $200 — 225
Page 41
    (a) . . . . $185 — 200
    (b) . . . . each, set of 6* $85 — 100
Page 42
    (a) . . . . each, set of 6* $75 — 95
    (b) . . . . each, set of 6* $65 — 85
    (c) . . . . each, set of 6* $65 — 85
Page 43
    (a) . . . . each, set of 6* $195 — 225
    (b) . . . . each, set of 6* $150 — 175
    (c) . . . . each, set of 6* $85 — 95
    (d) . . . . $100 — 135
Page 44
    (a) . . . . U.S. — each, set of 6* $135 — 150
    Canada — each, set of 6* $250 — 275
    (b) . . . . $235 — 250
Page 45
    (a) . . . . $165 — 185
    (b) . . . . each, set of 6* $125 — 135
Page 46
    (a) . . . . $265 — 285
    (b) . . . . $175 — 195
    (c) . . . . $195 — 225
    (d) . . . . $195 — 225
Page 47
    (a) . . . . $365 — 385
    (b) . . . . $385 — 395
    (c) . . . . $265 — 285
    (d) . . . . $195 — 225
Page 48 . . . . $225 — 245
Page 49
    (a) . . . . $195 — 225
    (b) . . . . $285 — 300
    (c) . . . . $265 — 285
    (d) . . . . $245 — 265
Page 50
    (a) . . . . $195 — 225
    (b) . . . . $235 — 250
Page 51
    (a) . . . . $195 — 235
    (b) . . . . $235 — 250
    (c) . . . . $195 — 235
    (d) . . . . $265 — 285
Page 52
    (a) . . . . $195 — 225
    (b) . . . . $285 — 300

* Unit prices are for chairs purchased in sets of 6. Chairs bought singly are usually priced considerably lower.

** Add $15 - 20 per additional leaf.

Value Guide
THE MARKETPLACE GUIDE TO
OAK FURNITURE Styles & Values
Copyright© 1980 by Peter S. Blundell
This book or any part thereof may not be reproduced
without the written consent of the author and publisher.
Published simultaneously in Canada by Thorncliffe House Inc.

Published by

COLLECTOR BOOKS   Box 3009   Paducah, Kentucky 42001

Printed in Canada